Huna - Discovering the Path to Your Silence

Huna, Volume 1

Katarzyna Biedrzycka

Published by Katarzyna Biedrzycka, 2024.

HUNA - DISCOVERING THE PATH TO YOUR SILENCE

First edition. February 12, 2024.

Copyright © 2024 Katarzyna Biedrzycka.

ISBN: 979-8224682263

Written by Katarzyna Biedrzycka.

Introduction

What is Huna?

Defining Huna is not straightforward. Throughout my research, I have encountered various assertions, each attempting to briefly and concisely capture its essence. Most commonly, these definitions touch on aspects of psychological and philosophical systems. While this is to some extent agreeable, Huna encompasses far more. Its perception is deeply personal, shaped by your openness to change, your maturity, and your current stage of development. There could be additional interpretations, but initially, Huna presents itself as a tool. It aids in transforming thought processes and perceptions of reality, leading to the dissolution of limiting beliefs and deep-seated programs, including those rooted in childhood.

From my perspective as a woman and a researcher, Huna transcends these basic definitions. I perceive it as a multifaceted healing system, encompassing various levels of energy and layers of existence – not just the physical body and the immediate reality. By following the path of Huna, you will develop an attitude of perceiving the good in yourself and in the surrounding world. Focus on that. This doesn't mean that you should silence or avoid external information. That would be rather unrealistic; besides, I appreciate being informed about what's happening in the system we are a part of. You'll transform into a passive observer of these processes and events. The greatest asset that every person possesses—their own energy—will be directed by you to where it can foster your satisfaction, fulfillment, health, and prosperity. Eventually, this will become a habit, a very positive one. Huna empowers you to be present in your experiences because our life is about our experiences, or rather, our constant experiencing.

You might ask, 'Am I not present now?' Most of us operate in a schematic manner throughout the day, performing repetitive activities: work, shopping, dinner, bath, sleep. Occasionally, on weekends or holidays, something different, deviating from our daily routine, emerges. Being present in your experience allows you to delve deeper, to see and understand more. Huna will help unearth your inner treasures and resources.

You might find yourself returning to childhood passions, pursuing long-abandoned intentions for which, miraculously, both the means and time will now appear. Each of us arrives in this world with specific gifts and purposes. We are spiritual beings, yet on Earth, we are meant to experience matter, to find ourselves within it, using all our capabilities and acting with respect for life and free will. This is our primary goal.

Initially, we are equipped with the necessary tools for this journey. However, over time, influenced by our unaware parents, education, religion, and various systems of supervision and control – both overt and hidden – we become programmed to forget these tools, to neglect their use.

Subsequently, we become a mass that is easily controlled and directed. Huna rekindles an awareness of our own power and value, opening up vast spaces within our hearts. This awakening serves to enhance the quality of life on multiple levels. Perhaps the most challenging aspect to convey is the simplicity of Huna. :) Adopting it into your daily life will reveal its logical, yet clear and transparent nature. It helps you understand the consequences of your choices, illuminating why you made a particular decision over another. You will begin to practically harness the unlimited powers of your mind. At its core, Huna is knowledge about life, its causes, and effects. It reminds us of the fundamental principles that underpin our existence in this reality.

You'll likely agree that the 20th century witnessed a profound revolution in experimental physics, leading to the advent of quantum physics. Irrefutable research has demonstrated that what we perceive as matter is, in the universe, merely more or less condensed vibrating energy. In Huna, theory gives way to practice, and blind faith is superseded by knowledge. This knowledge creates a bridge between the ancient teachings of the kahunas and quantum physics.

The functioning of the invisible spiritual world is highly tangible. Each of us is the creator of our next day, continuously shaping it, whether we realize it or not.

Isn't it better to do this consciously? To move towards our goals effortlessly, without struggling with life, with ourselves, with our thoughts. Remember, you are not just a physical being, a mere amalgamation of chemical processes governed solely by the laws of physics. You are a powerful energetic entity, inhabiting this physical form for a purpose – to experience through the senses, to navigate the world we live in. The potential for growth and flourishing within you is boundless. It doesn't matter if you can't see it right now. For many years, numerous systems and institutions have exerted great effort to lull your spiritual being into slumber.

To distort, obscure, and transform your understanding of the energetic-spiritual realm. You were conditioned to prioritize materialism and adhere to prescribed norms. You were taught what to think, not how to think; when to feel, not how to spontaneously flow with the signals from your own heart. But now, this is changing. Give yourself a chance.

'Huna' is a Hawaiian word meaning 'secret' or 'hidden'. Yet, there's nothing mysterious about it; Huna is the innate power within us all, always ready to be actualized in reality. The free will of every individual dictates whether they will fully embrace and utilize their inherent powers, or remain dormant in their awareness. The choice is yours.

History of Huna

Over the years, I have encountered many versions of Huna's history. Some trace its origins back to ancient Egypt, while others suggest it's a legacy of the lost Atlantis, preserved for the benefit of humanity. There are also theories proposing that Huna's teachings were imparted by the Pleiadians. Certain sources refer to 12 tribes that once inhabited the Sahara when it was a lush, fertile paradise. These tribes were believed to be of high spiritual development and, as environmental conditions changed, they migrated to regions like the Atlas Mountains and Polynesia. It's said that there, they settled and entrusted their profound magical knowledge to select individuals.

Let's set aside these diverse historical threads and venture a bit further. Picture one of the stunning Polynesian islands, untouched by the trappings of modern civilization. Here, simple yet contented people lived in peaceful harmony with the rhythms of nature.

Women managed the households and cared for the children, while the men engaged in hunting and tackled the more strenuous tasks. Among these men, some possessed healing abilities, and their counsel often led to positive outcomes, resolving various problems. These individuals weren't formally educated in the conventional sense, but their understanding of the human psyche was extraordinarily advanced, surpassing what is typically taught in modern universities. They were known as 'kahunas', a term that literally means 'keeper of the secret.'

These kahunas were individuals who consciously wielded great power to aid others. Despite the high regard in which they were held, they remained grounded, living at the same level as their fellow tribespeople. As time flowed on, this profound knowledge was transferred orally from one generation to the next. Periodically, guided by their own discernment, kahunas would select certain children from the village.

From their early years, these selected children were nurtured and educated in the spirit of Huna. They delved into the intricate relationships among humans, animals, and nature. They were taught to cultivate a harmonious cooperation between their three selves, which in today's terms would be identified as the conscious, subconscious, and superconscious. Central to their education was the principle of unity with other people and with nature, forming the cornerstone of their teachings and practices. In this way, a new generation of kahunas was cultivated.

However, the year 1820 marked a significant shift. European ships arrived on one of the islands, introducing an alien civilization to the natives, along with a new religious doctrine — Christianity. As time progressed, the islands underwent further development. Newcomers arrived from distant lands, transforming the living spaces of the natives. Despite these changes, the teachings of Huna continued to be orally transmitted to successive generations.

The kahunas remained dedicated to their role, offering healing not just for the body, but for the mind and spirit as well.

As the presence of the Catholic Church grew on the islands, its priests and clergy began to feel increasingly threatened.

Their rites and practices did not seem to match the effectiveness of the kahunas' methods. Consequently, more and more islanders began to prefer the guidance and assistance of these tribal shamans over the church's representatives. In response to their diminishing influence, the church's authorities labeled the practices of the kahunas as black magic. They warned the people of dire consequences and punishments for following these ancient traditions. Under this mounting pressure and condemnation, the healing and helping practices rooted in Huna wisdom were eventually outlawed. As a result, Huna was forced into secrecy, continuing its existence in the shadows.

Despite the restrictions, Huna persisted, stealthily handed down through generations. Its clandestine journey through time was interrupted in 1917 when Max Freedom Long, a young American, arrived on one of the Hawaiian Islands. A psychology student, teacher, and member of the Theosophical Society, Long was destined to become the first person to decode Huna for the Western world – but that part of the story comes later. While working in a Hawaiian school, he stumbled upon the local healing practices. Struck by the effectiveness of a kahuna's methods, he found himself drawn into the world of native culture and customs.

Long spent considerable time in the villages, engaging in conversations and learning, intrigued by their enigmatic language and practices. He observed that the locals employed a specific verbal code, one they were hesitant to share with outsiders. This intrigue fueled his dedication, leading him to devote over 50 years of his life to uncovering the secrets of this elusive knowledge. Through his extensive research, Long discovered that the kahunas, in their healing prayers, addressed a specific part of the human mind, akin to what is understood in modern psychology therapies. They had the ability to identify subconscious blockages and foster a spiritual union of a person's three selves.

Starting in 1936, Max Freedom Long began publishing a series of books on Huna, encapsulating the wisdom accrued over five decades of research and practice. He continued his work until his death in 1971. Long bequeathed his vast collection of documentation and his entire library to Dolly Ware, a dedicated student of Huna and the curator of the Max Freedom Long Library.

The Construction of the Human Psyche According to Huna

The Three Selves of a Human

The concept of the "Three Selves of Man" in Huna can be traced back to ancient beliefs, with its roots found in the traditions of the Assyrians and Babylonians. This tripartite idea is also echoed in Egyptian hieroglyphs and pictorial writings, and parallels can be drawn to the religions and psychological teachings of figures like Freud and Jung. While psychology as a formal science began to take shape around 1880, the kahunas, long before this, were adept in recognizing and utilizing three distinct aspects of consciousness. They possessed a deep understanding of the function, actions, and motivations of each aspect, recognizing that together, these components comprise the full spectrum of the human being.

According to Huna, every individual harbors three levels of consciousness, each interconnected:

1. The Lower Self or subconscious,
2. The Middle Self or consciousness,
3. The Higher Self or superconsciousness.

Each level has its unique function and motivation, but in essence, they are unified and share a common origin. By restoring free communication and cooperation among these three selves, one can achieve a holistic perspective of the world and daily life.

This integration enables the full realization of an individual's physical, mental, and spiritual potential.

The Lower Self, namely the Subconscious

Each of us, in addition to having a physical body, also possesses subtle bodies, commonly referred to as an aura. This aura, vibrating at a higher frequency than physical matter, is not usually perceptible to our standard senses. People who can see human auras describe them as multi-layered energetic fields pulsating with colors. The variety and intensity of these colors are reflective of our mood and health. The Lower Self is associated with the etheric body, a state that exists between energy and matter, mirroring the structure of the physical body, including all anatomical parts and organs. At this density, on this vibrational level, an exchange of energy occurs among different beings, including humans and animals.

The subconscious communicates with us through dreams, feelings, premonitions, imagination, and spontaneous daydreams. It is responsible for telepathy and clairvoyance. Everything that reaches us from the external world first passes through our Lower Self. When the Lower Self receives a signal from reality, from our surroundings, it does not judge or classify it. Instead, it passes the signal to the Middle Self, which then assesses its significance. It is only after this assessment that the emotions associated with the signal are recorded. The more significant an event is to us, the more intensely and enduringly it is remembered—be it fears, anxieties, traumatic scenes, or emotions related to love, joy, and delight. If you ever encounter a similar event, your initial reaction will be rekindled. Realizing that your emotional state depends largely on you, on your habits and preferences (which can be changed and transformed), will significantly enhance the quality of your life. Above all, it will contribute to regaining your health. It is crucial that our Lower Self is free from unfavorable programs. This area also encompasses our genetic memory and the memories of past incarnations. Our memories and experiences, both conscious and unconscious, are housed in our Lower Self. This includes habits, beliefs, programs, and suggestions accumulated throughout life from various influences such as parents, caregivers, education, religious systems, and even the media we consume. The subconscious is capable of learning and adapting. For instance, driving a car becomes almost automatic over time as the actions are performed subconsciously. The Lower Self also plays a crucial role in maintaining our body's vital functions, overseeing involuntary activities like heartbeat and breathing. We are inherently designed to live in health, but negative programs and emotions can often disrupt our body's balance. The Lower Self interprets things literally and responds to autosuggestions and suggestions. Therefore, formulating positive affirmations and changes with care is essential, as the Lower Self does not distinguish between jest and seriousness.

Building a loving connection with our Lower Self is crucial for understanding and applying the principles of Huna, ultimately leading to control over various aspects of our life. The Lower Self thrives on learning, playing, and requires a nurturing environment filled with love, akin to befriending the five-year-old child within us. Gentle yet firm suggestions, conveyed in a playful and loving manner, can be highly effective.

Before moving forward, take a moment to ask yourself a few questions and observe the emotions that arise with the answers. Allow the answers to surface naturally, without forcing them:

1. How often do you experience 'guilt'?
2. How often do you encounter negative emotions?
3. Do you understand your behaviors?
4. Do you trust your intuition?
5. Do you feel that your life is on the right track?

Now, picture a chair opposite you. Sitting on it is a five-year-old child – that's you at five. As you gaze into each other's eyes, what do you feel compelled to do?"

The Middle Self, namely Consciousness

The Middle Self is the aspect of self that you identify as "I". It encompasses your personality, character, logical reasoning, analysis, and the processing of facts. This level of consciousness enables you to communicate, learn, develop, and make decisions. It is the source of judgment and comparison. Unlike the Lower Self, the Middle Self does not possess memory or emotions; it operates based on facts, logical conclusions, and experimental findings. Functioning predominantly in the present, it is able to distinguish the past, future, and present, yet it does not form habits. The Middle Self reacts to life's events using subconscious programs and evaluates and interprets stimuli from the external world during everyday activities. With its capacity for free will and abstract thinking, the Middle Self can conceptualize what does not yet exist, in contrast to the subconscious, which can only reimagine what already exists. Thus, it is the Middle Self that should guide and supervise the subconscious. By consciously directing energy with your Middle Self, as energy follows attention, you can actively shape your reality. In this sense, the rational, logical mind serves as a guide and supervisor for the Lower Self.

Higher Self, namely Superconsciousness

According to Huna, each of us harbors within a divine part, a divine spark – the higher self of our being, where the feminine and masculine elements are harmoniously integrated. Huna priests did not regard the higher self as the ultimate God but rather described it as a spiritual parent, akin to a guardian. This concept is similar to the notion of a guardian angel in Christianity. Ultimately, the specific name is of little consequence; what's important is that it represents that part of you which connects with higher energies, with the energy of love from the Creator in the act of creation. It's a realm of beauty and universal love. Whether you believe in it, acknowledge it, or utilize it, its existence remains unaffected. It is always there, accompanying you until your last breath, and then it participates in the ongoing process of growth. This part of yourself is fully developed, existing in a state of constant happiness and fulfillment. As you read these words through your Middle Self, your consciousness, your subconscious may stir up emotions. However, the essence of the Higher Self cannot be fully grasped by the mind; it is an intuitive understanding, a precious gift bestowed upon every person. Kahunas did not seek to intellectually understand this; they neither created religions nor philosophical theories around it. Instead, they simply felt and knew. Your superconsciousness operates on such a subtle level that lower vibrations like anger, sadness, revenge, and pain have no place in it. The Higher Self is incapable of causing harm or damage and demands nothing from you – no sacrifices, gifts, or the burning of magical candles or altars. Without these, it can guide you towards the best and happiest path in this life, in this reality. Yet, it does not interfere with the free will of the consciousness, remaining a passive observer unless invited into your life. Opening this channel of communication connects you with a supportive, inspiring, protective, and loving spiritual guardian. All it takes is to open yourself to its assistance and trust. The Higher Self does not issue commands; its voice is a quiet whisper, heard in your soul or heart, bringing knowledge accompanied by a sense of peace and subtle excitement. The Higher Self cannot be persuaded or bribed; it is in tune with your perfect divine plan, your ideal model of reality.

It is not a wish-granting genie; achieving full symbiosis among your three selves and understanding the process of directing and managing your own energy are necessary. However, it can serve as an inspiration and guide, aligned with the pattern of your ideal reality. Trusting in and unblocking the paths between your selves can lead to miraculous events. The Higher Selves of all people are interconnected, forming a unity. Therefore, harming others is, in essence, harming oneself. In Huna, the only wrongdoing is the intentional causing of harm to another being. Good communication with your Higher Self is facilitated through the subconscious, which communicates with your guardian spirit, while the consciousness is necessary to define, specify, and direct. These channels of communication should remain clear and undisturbed, maintaining a state of symbiosis.

Do you recall a moment in your life when something occurred that could be described as a 'miracle' or a 'wonderful coincidence'?

Have you ever felt as though someone or something is watching over you? That perhaps providence is protecting and guiding you?

Building and Strengthening the Connection with the Lower Self

Your lower self, your subconscious, is a powerful ally in the process of healing, shaping reality, and realizing desires and intentions. This is only possible with good communication and an open, sincere connection. You might not even realize how many blocked and suppressed emotions you carry within. Sometimes they emerge as spontaneous tears when a scene in a movie reminds you of a childhood episode. At such moments, your subconscious might surface the face of your mother or father, unspoken words or those that should never have been said, causing a tightening in the throat, a pain in the solar plexus. How many times has your lower self called out to you in this way?

Events like these indicate areas that need to be cleared and healed, accepted, perhaps forgiven and let go. Negative emotions such as anger, regret, hatred, rage, sadness, and despair reside within, constantly being pushed into oblivion. But the subconscious does not forget. If something has left a significant emotional imprint on it, it will periodically bring this to the surface, crying out, 'Do something about this.'

The subconscious does not distinguish between past and present. Therefore, every memory or feeling that you bring to your awareness affects your body. It makes no difference whether the event is happening now or occurred 15 years ago; the subconscious reacts according to the situation currently being processed in your mind. Constantly dwelling on old wounds and grievances is not the best idea. Suppressing these negative emotions, sometimes for many years, can lead to chronic autoimmune diseases when the body, driven by a sense of guilt, wants to punish itself. Tumors and growths appear on the body. The liver begins to fail. This energy simply seeks an outlet. It's like living on an active volcano. You never know when it will erupt.

Your subconscious, as long as you breathe, will always strive for homeostasis in the body, to restore balance and health. Help it in this process, understand how it functions. Clear and work through the difficult situations from your life, and finally, take a breath. Then, just don't hinder it. Pay attention to what you put into your body, what foods you eat. Get enough sleep and move as much as you can. Love, give, and receive love. Even older individuals should be as physically active as their bodies and medical assessments allow.

In the following chapters of the book, I will suggest how you can deal with difficult emotions or traumas from the past. Your lower self can do a lot for you; a good connection with it can transform your life beyond recognition. However, your path must be clear, communication effective, and trust a natural feeling. You will be most effective in influencing your lower self when you are completely relaxed.

HUNA - DISCOVERING THE PATH TO YOUR SILENCE

Find a moment in the day when you no longer have to perform any duties or tasks. Turn off your phone, computer, and TV. Make sure that no one will disturb you, and reconnect with your lower self.

Lie down or sit, making sure you are comfortable and warm. Try to feel your body with your eyes closed. Imagine that you are surrounded by a sphere of white-golden light, knowing it's the positive energy of love. It envelops you and your space. With your 'inner eye', locate any muscle tension. As you focus on this, you will feel it more distinctly. Relax these tensions without moving your body, simply issue a command to relax, like, 'now the tension is leaving my shoulders.' Check if you are relaxed yet, take as much time as you need, don't rush. With your eyes still closed, try to look at the point between your eyebrows. Try to maintain this gaze. Ask your lower self a question in your inner voice (or say it out loud if you can). What is it? Ask it to show you its image.

The first thing you see with your inner insight comes from your subconscious. You might see yourself at around 3—6 years of age, an animal, or some symbol like a geometric figure. Ask your lower self if it wants you to address it by a specific name. If such information comes, remember it. Pay attention to the emotions you are feeling. Tell your subconscious that you are rebuilding your relationship, that you really want this and are happy about it.

Repeat this exercise periodically, solely to strengthen your connection. From now on, call upon your lower self using the information you received, the image, and perhaps a name.

No :) what I have just described is not a prelude to personality disintegration or schizophrenia, but rather the rebuilding of the access path to your subconscious. Trust your feelings; if this resonates with you and you feel comfortable with it, then it means it's right for you.

Experiencing Reality According to Huna

THE KAHUNAS KNEW THAT material reality is not the only reality in which we function as a whole self. They divided the entire process into four structures of beliefs about our experience. The first level is objective, material. You experience it through your senses and analyze it with your mind. On this basis, the scientific system and Western civilization developed. The conception of this level involves separating 'me, you, this, that,' thereby allowing us the possibility of direct, sensory experience. This, in turn, allowed for the development of industry, technology, and philosophy. In this level of experience, if something has a beginning, it must also have an end. The structures prevailing here are so obvious, manifest, and logical that it's hard to believe another reality might exist.

The second level was defined as subjective. To experience here, one must develop intuition and emotional intelligence. This is the realm of dreams, clairvoyance, clairaudience. It forms the backdrop for your lower self. Here you can work with your energies and emotions most effectively. It's important to notice the moment when these two levels intersect and how a change in one affects the other.

The third level is the world of symbols and archetypes. The kahunas knew that everything is symbolic in this space. Experiences are a reflection of your 'Self.' All things, people, animals are your mirror. Here, everything has the meaning you give to it. Many cultures have developed systems of symbolic knowledge to peer into this invisible, subtle world. Meanings were attributed to signs. Runes, Kabbalah, I Ching, and many others.

The fourth level is holistic reality. It's a state of highly developed consciousness, of being one with the universe. Here, everything is one. To heal and help people effectively, the kahunas had integrated the three levels of their self - the lower, middle, and higher selves working in symbiosis.

They also freely moved between the four described realities, altering the specific experience they were working on.

Main Principles of Huna

IN THIS CHAPTER, THE simplicity of Huna will be presented, and the beauty of this simplicity. Seven principles that do not conflict with any religion or creed, impose nothing, and require nothing. By analyzing them, you will understand how the internal causes of your external events manifest. Here you will find the latest discoveries in quantum physics, explained in simple words without formulas and complex calculations. The principles of Huna can be an inspiration for your own reflections. You will accept them to the extent that your openness allows, to see the extraordinary in ordinary reality.

IKE

THE WORLD IS WHAT YOU think it is. This is the foundation of the entire Huna philosophy, Beliefs, patterns, ways of thinking, attitudes, significant experiences, fears — all these have so far shaped your worldview. What you see now in your reality is the result of many years of work, starting from childhood. Do you like what you see? Does your path serve you well? Is it pleasant and friendly? Let's consider: if, according to Huna, my world is as I think of it, can changing my thought pattern change my reality? Yes, if you consciously change your thought patterns, your habits and customs will change. You will start to decide which thoughts to let flow freely and which to let go and drift away. Managing your thoughts is easy — if you decide so. It's a collaboration between the middle and lower self. In the surrounding reality, new events, people, reactions, circumstances, and life conditions will emerge. Changing the way of thinking can apply to every aspect of your daily life, if it requires it.

Let's assume that your body is underperforming and suffering from some chronic illness. You think about it, focus on it, analyze test results, search for information on medications, discuss it with family and friends, read forums where people with similar problems share their experiences, look for a miraculous diet, the perfect supplements, and before sleep, you construct a bleak scenario in your mind. Do you realize how much energy you have put into your illness? You are 'feeding' it. Emotions arise in this process. Fear, anxiety, perhaps anger. In such a situation, your lower self will do much to ensure that this illness occupies as much space in your life as possible. You bring it to life through your thoughts, speech, emotions. You might ask: so what should I do? Pretend it doesn't exist? — I can't do that. Don't pretend, you can't fool yourself. Change the polarity from negative to positive. Continue all the activities as you have been doing. Follow your doctor's advice, take care of yourself, undergo tests if necessary, but do it as if you were going to check the mailbox, impassively.

Talk to people who build your positivity, read information that brings joy, surround yourself only with those people in whose company you feel good, work with your lower self, you now need to accustom it to a different thought pattern. You can use affirmations, autosuggestion, visualizations, which hold immense power. And what about fear? Your freedom begins where fear ends. You can change a lot, as the next principle of Huna will explain. Choose wisely, because your life operates on the principle of 'say and you shall have' :)

KALA

There are no limits. According to the teachings of Huna, you are an infinite being in an infinite universe, which is a field of unlimited possibilities. At a certain stage of your growth, you chose to 'experience' matter, which is why you find yourself here, in this space, taking on this physical body. To create an experience, certain boundaries are necessary. You cannot experience 'something' in infinity. It needs to be narrowed down, condensed. This allows you to continue developing as a being of the universe, expanding your self-awareness, perception of observation, reminding yourself of who you truly are, and what you are capable of. Experiencing this is much more than just knowledge. The kahunas believe that everything is interconnected, and since you are a part of the universe with unlimited possibilities, you have the right to make use of it. Where, then, do all these blockages within us come from? They are programs embedded in your lower self. Their origins may trace back to early childhood. Often, we are unaware of these processes and how much they disrupt and complicate our lives.

We fail to realize that the reason for our suffering may be negative beliefs. These beliefs will attract situations into our life that confirm them. I once knew a person who often used the phrase 'I don't believe in miracles' in casual conversation. I think that in their life, no miraculous coincidence can occur because their mind does not even allow for such a possibility. They are limiting their own reality. These blockages stem only from our limited views, habits, beliefs, customs, fears. Find and change these subconscious limiting patterns within you, and you will see how quickly the space around you changes. What previously hindered development, expression, and growth will dissolve. The universe is a field of unlimited possibilities, open yourself up to it.

MAKIA

Energy follows attention. Recent developments in quantum physics have proven to us that everything is energy. One could say that a human is an energetic-vibrational generator of various frequencies. Most diseases and failures are disturbances in this field, and we can always work on that. Thought is energy, fields of vibrating energy. They influence matter, your reality. Whether you want it or not doesn't matter. When you focus your thoughts on a certain topic, a collection of them forms and creates so-called thought-forms. You 'feed' them with your energy because that's where your attention is now directed. An energetic entity with a specific vibrational field is created. If your thoughts revolve around a happy and pleasant subject, the vibrations are at a higher level. If you worry, are sad, or angry, a thought-form with low vibrations is created. However, what is important is that they will attract events and people who emit the same or similar vibration to yours. What you send out comes back. And no one judges whether it is good or bad for you. You are responsible for this process. It's worth knowing that we possess such power — what you dedicate your attention to grows and manifests in your life. You also possess free will, and by using it, you can direct your energy. There is also the opposite pole of this 'superpower' of ours :) If you have already created negative, low-vibrating thought-forms, like an illness, conflict, or scarcity — don't fight them. Stop feeding them with your energy, don't send your attention there. Over time, they will fall away, wither, and disappear from your space. It's valuable to be a conscious creator and respect your energy. Send it where it serves you and builds a joyful everyday life. Always focus solely on what you want to achieve. In the later part of the book, we will practice focusing the middle and lower self on the same thought object, at the same time.

MANAWA

The Power of Now is in the Present Moment. Here and now. We are accustomed to dividing years into months, days, hours, minutes. We define our lives by the past, present, and future. We live with memories of the past, both good and bad, and we plan for the future. We wonder what we will do tomorrow, next month, next year. But where is the present moment? What is it? It is your moment of power. By dwelling, for instance, on a painful past, you are merely interpreting those events in the present. They no longer exist. If you allow them to dominate your mind and your present, you become their victim. You lose your power. If you understand this, your lower self will adopt a new thought program, and you can then rid yourself of the tormenting emotions associated with a situation that no longer exists. View it as something that has passed. Even the most painful experiences served a purpose, often only realized after many, many years. Only you have the power within yourself to change the limiting blockages and beliefs at this very moment. Only you and only now. And what about the future? People who live with the belief in the unchangeability of fate, karma, and inevitable destiny are depriving themselves of power. I don't question the existence of these concepts, but I know we have a significant influence on this process. If you consciously change this belief, you will find many opportunities to make positive changes in these areas. We can never be one hundred percent certain of what will happen tomorrow; we only make logical conclusions or intuitive hypotheses. However, we can greatly influence this by recognizing opportunities that exist here and now.

ALOHA

Love is meant to bring happiness. Can we understand the spirit of aloha as the kahunas did? Observing themselves and the space around them, they saw the 'spark of the Creator' in everything. In the current of a rushing river, in a stone lying on the beach, in the leaves at the top of trees, in animals. They knew that we are all connected, that we are one. If we look today at how the universe functions, how the human body works, if we observe nature and animals living in the wild — one thought becomes apparent: all of this originated from love. The power of this energy is unimaginable. It is the power of building, healing, purifying. We often call this state universal love — towards oneself, towards others, towards animals, plants, and the space in which we function. It is closeness without expectations, demands, commands, or prohibitions, without contracts and oaths. Love is freedom.

MANA

All power comes from within. People often look for power in the external world. I did the same for half of my life. We seek support, consolation, strength, help, love, God... outside. Everything you experience, you experience only in your own field, and you can only change your field by yourself. Every change originates from within you. You are the greatest source of power for yourself; no one and nothing has a greater impact on your life than you do. Unless you decide otherwise. Mana is the creative force of the universe, the force of creation that permeates everything, and when combined with human free will, it becomes a powerful 'tool' for making changes in one's own life. You can change much, your relationships with loved ones, your body, your everyday surroundings, if only you reclaim the right and power to manage your own energy and to consciously shape reality, starting from this moment.

PONO

Effectiveness is the measure of truth. If something works for you, brings happiness, fulfillment, a sense of accomplishment, and is effective, then it means it's worth holding onto, worth developing, worth continuing. It is true for you. However, it's important to remember that your actions should be in line with the spirit of aloha. Intentionally harming another being, whether mentally, physically, or emotionally, is the only transgression in Huna. The more you grow in understanding of the power behind these simple principles, the more capable you will become of creating your own reality in the way you desire.

Types and Functions of Life Energy

A key concept in Huna is mana. It is energy, vital force, prana, the universal life force. Mana is indeed energy, necessary for life. It pulsates in every being, in every plant. It is the basis of all processes of thinking, expanding consciousness, and all life functions of every organism. Every human body is filled with energy that participates in cycles of energetic exchange. Mana is in the air, though it is not air itself. It is in matter, but it is not matter. It is in food, but not any of the substances that make up nourishment. It is in water, but it is not water. It is in sunlight, but it is not the light of its rays. To the kahunas, it was identified with water. Like water, it can flow freely or its flow can be blocked. It can be stored and used when needed.

A very important element in the practice of Huna is proper breathing, and it is closely connected with the absorption of mana. The initial exercises should involve combining these two elements. This will achieve internal balance, integrate the selves, clear the blockages of your energy system, and increase its potential. If you want to change a space in your reality and supply this imagination with a lot of mana, then it has greater power and more influence on your material world. Replenishing energy in the body is a natural function of the lower self. It does this with every breath. If the subconscious is accustomed to shallow and unstable breathing, then it draws little energy. If the breath is full and calm, then our body is supplied with a greater amount of it. It's worth knowing that as you practice Huna, your energetic potential grows. The impact on the surroundings becomes greater, and the creation of reality occurs freely.

MANA

Mana is the space of our lower self. Replenishing energy in the body is its natural function, and it does this with each of our breaths. If your breathing is shallow and unstable, you cannot provide yourself with a sufficient amount of energy. We tend to breathe faster and more superficially, using only the upper part of our lungs. A lack of mana significantly lowers your well-being, leading to diseases, depression, anxiety disorders; you lack the desire for anything, and nothing brings you joy. Conscious, proper breathing will make a huge impression on your lower self, capture its attention, and you will feel it yourself during the first exercise. Familiarize yourself with diaphragmatic breathing; it helps reduce tension and stress and accustoms the lower self to correct breathing. At the beginning of breathing exercises, do not exceed 5–10 minutes, approach body energizing carefully if you have never done it before. Over time, your energy capacity will increase, and your body will become accustomed to a greater potential.

Exercise

Find a comfortable position for yourself, you can sit or lie down. It's important that your spine is straight and that you feel warm and comfortable. Try to relax. Surround yourself with a sphere of white-golden light, knowing that it's the positive energy of love. It envelops you and your space. If various thoughts and images come to mind, allow them for a moment. Now, begin to observe your breath. Don't control it, don't change it, just observe. Notice if there are any sensations flowing from your body, locate any tensions, you will feel them. Now, with each inhale, focus on the top of your head, only during the inhale. Breathe like this for a while. Let your breath be free, don't direct it. Now, with each exhale, focus on the base of your spine, where the tailbone is. Now you shift your attention from the inhale to the exhale. Breathe like this for a while. We will combine these two processes: on the inhale, focus on the top of your head; on the exhale, focus on the base of the spine. Breathe in this manner for a while, and then return to your natural breathing.

It is beneficial to repeat this exercise, gradually extending the relaxation time. Over time, we can add visualization. On the inhale, imagine the sun's rays illuminating the top of our head and filling us with mana, positive good energy. While charging with mana, it is always good to visualize pure and luminous energy. During the exhale, we can visualize all that is unnecessary, unneeded, and detrimental leaving our body, exiting through the base of the spine.

Exercise for Releasing Negative Patterns, Events, and Emotional Traumas. Start this exercise once you have mastered the previous one.

Find a comfortable position for yourself, you can sit or lie down. It's important that your spine is straight and that you feel warm and comfortable. Surround yourself with a sphere of white-golden light, knowing that it's the positive energy of love. It envelops you and your space.

Bring to mind what you want to release. Try to visualize it as realistically as possible. If you need to return to unpleasant past events, do so. For a moment, you may feel emotional discomfort or tears may flow, don't worry about it. Focus on your body and see where this emotion has settled, the first sensation is true, don't force the search. You may physically feel it, or your lower self may show you, for example, a red fiery ball around the liver or a dark unpleasant sludge around the shoulders. This is a very individual process. Once you locate the unwanted pattern in your body, with each inhale, send light there, cleansing mana. Dissolve, melt, wash away. Use whatever resonates with you most at the moment. Each exhale frees you from what the inhale has cleansed. Do this for a while, you'll feel when to stop. Once you return to your normal breathing, imagine your life or yourself free from this pattern.

Repeat this exercise as often as needed until the place you've located appears free, clean, filled with light. Nature is very willing to share mana with us. Whenever you can, walk in the forest, meadows, by lakes, the sea, or in the mountains. If it's warm, take off your shoes and walk barefoot. Touch the earth, trees, stones with the intention of receiving energetic support. The sun is a wonderful giver of mana. Gradually accustom your skin to the sunlight to avoid burns, but never avoid the sun.

Mana – mana

The kahunas called this type of mana 'nourishment for the middle self.' Basic mana splits into two, allowing our consciousness to function efficiently, to think, reason, create imaginations, realize, and use our intelligence. When the level of mana-mana is low, the middle self may lose control over our lower self. This can be quite dangerous and may lead to unpleasant consequences. The subconscious, left unsupervised, behaves chaotically and unrestrainedly. This can lead to difficult addictions, depressions, and diseases stemming from emotional dysfunction. By doubling the word mana, the kahunas also understood the doubling of its power, necessary to persuade the lower self to cooperate in solving and eliminating problems. Today, we might call this strong will or the power of consciousness. With a high level of life energy, it is easier to control one's will, for example, in getting rid of addictions, phobias, or depression.

Mana – loa

There is also a type of mana associated with our higher self. Mana-loa, a high vibration of happiness, love, bliss. The highest energy with transformative ability. This is an immensely powerful energy. It is through this that 'miraculous healings' or other processes that we know as 'miracles' occur. When you integrate your three selves, when they create a symbiosis in cooperation, you will know its power. A feeling you will never forget, difficult to describe. Mana-loa is energy received from the higher self, flowing through you like a powerful positive force. The materialization of your intentions is effortless, regardless of the obstacles you may encounter along the way. The results of creation are quick and certain. We will discuss this more in the context of Huna prayer.

Telepathic Connections — 'Aka Threads'

According to Huna teachings, communication between the selves occurs through aka threads, which are telepathic connections used by our lower self. These should be continuously nurtured and expanded as our consciousness develops. These connections occur between the lower self and the middle self, and between the lower self and the higher self. The topic is not limited to this communication alone. If you come into contact with anything through your senses, you automatically create aka threads, which you can use in the future. Only the subconscious knows how to use these threads, and it can connect through them with various things or people.

Physics describes this phenomenon as quantum entanglement. Experiments and research have shown that if two objects interact and then separate, they remain under each other's influence. Imagine thin threads, like a spider's web, made of invisible matter, connecting you to everything you pay attention to or touch. Time or distance does not matter here, nor do physical objects limit the channel of this transmission. These delicate, invisible aka threads, however, have no greater significance or value to us until we start to energize them. We can stimulate them with our consciousness; they then tense up, becoming strong and powerful.

Imagine how strong these connections can be when a mother can telepathically sense danger around her distant child. Or a couple in love — able to send this beautiful energy to each other from distant countries, and one side knows that the other is thinking or remembering them. This is their silent connection through an invisible communication channel. Along it flows a stream of life force, love. Thoughts or memories of one of the lovers stay in the sender's memory but are duplicated, and as duplicates, they travel to the receiver. When they reach the destination, the receiver's lower self transfers them to the consciousness center to be realized.

The more energy and love you devote to your aka threads, the more useful they will be for you. You can consciously create your own aka threads, strengthen them, or conversely, remove them. If you feel that a connection with a person or thing is detrimental to you, causing suffering or sadness, cut it off. Your sincere intention, the feeling of shedding a burden, and awareness of what you want to do have enormous power in this case.

Exercise

Enter a state of relaxation with your eyes closed. Surround yourself with a sphere of white-golden light, knowing that it is the positive energy of love. It envelops you and your space. In your imagination, summon the image of the person or thing from which you want to sever the connection. Now see how from the area around your navel, the seat of the subconscious, a thread emerges, connecting you to this person or thing. Thank them for all the experiences, even if you don't understand them now, even if they were painful. In a moment, you will release and let go of it. Imagine untying this thread or cutting it with scissors. See it moving away from you, disappearing into the distance. Gently come out of the relaxation and observe your feelings.

You can also send healing energy (mana) to a sick person in this way, or simply send love energy to a loved one who is far away.

Exercise

Enter a state of relaxation with your eyes closed. Surround yourself with a sphere of white-golden light, knowing that it is the positive energy of love. It envelops you and your space. In your imagination, bring forth the image of the person to whom you want to send love and supportive mana. Now see how from the area around your navel, the seat of the subconscious, a thread emerges, connecting you to this person. You can see it as a cord pulsating with the energy of love. With each breath, you send another packet of positive energy to the person you love. Visualize their face, see them smiling, knowing what they feel is coming from you. Gently come out of the relaxation and observe your feelings.

Blocked Communication Path Between the Selves

HOW MANY UNANSWERED prayers have there been in your life?

How many unfulfilled dreams?

How many abandoned plans?

We already know that the lower self is connected to the higher self through aka threads.

It is through these that communication occurs. For your actions and prayers to be effective, a clear path is necessary. Unhindered communication between the lower self, the consciousness, and the superconsciousness is essential. When is this path blocked? When you harbor negative thoughts, programs, fears, guilt, feelings of unworthiness, doubt. The kahunas referred to these negative programs as 'eating companions.' Quite an apt description considering that many people carry these with them throughout their lives. All our failures have their cause in the subconscious, which maintains these 'eating companions.' We also give these negative mental creatures our life energy, mana. A clear path is nothing but a clean subconscious. Free from complexes, feelings of unworthiness, guilt, pessimism, fears, uncertainties, and other detrimental things that reside in the lower self.

Unfortunately, the life we lead in our times and societies fosters the creation of these negative burdens. We are bombarded from all sides with demands, prohibitions, and commands, kept in a state of helplessness, despair, and low spiritual consciousness. We constantly fear ridicule and negative opinions from acquaintances, coworkers, and family. On the other hand, we are expected to achieve perfect results in work, education, and child-rearing. We should look perfect and always wear a smiling mask.

An inner rebellion arises. First quiet, but gradually gaining strength. Psychological tensions grow. We try to drown them out with addictions, escaping from ourselves, or seeking love anywhere outside. Medications for depression, calm, and sleep are distributed like candy at a market stall. You cannot silence these negative emotions for long until you understand what is happening to you, where it comes from, and how to deal with it.

I have already written that we are powerful spiritual beings in human bodies. Our souls will call within us to awaken and understand the power of our own might. You won't find this outside. Understand, clear, and calm your inner world, and gradually what is unfavorable around you will change. Among these negative programs I mentioned, two are particularly burdensome and toxic energetically. These are the feelings of guilt and unworthiness. Ultimately, one is linked to the other.

When your lower self harbors guilt, the communication path between the selves has been energetically blocked.

If you ever felt that you have wronged another being physically, mentally, or emotionally, your subconscious remembers that thought and feels guilty. Your lower self feels unworthy of experiencing the joy of life, love, and certainly not worthy of contact with the higher self. It doesn't feel deserving, it feels guilty. If such a situation occurred in your life and you know you have wronged someone, it can be rectified. The simplest way would be to ask for forgiveness from that person. However, I realize that this is not always so easy. It's possible that the person is no longer among the living. Through work with your subconscious and exercises, you can reach a state where it is convinced that it is free from this burden.

Many examples of blocked communication paths between the selves can be given beyond feelings of guilt, but let's consider conflicting imaginations for a moment. They too are a cause of failure.

What is your lower self's attitude towards wealth?
Can it be obtained only through hard, tedious work?
Are rich people certainly swindlers and schemers?
Can wealth be acquired from honest work?

On one hand, we want to live in abundance and strive for it, but on the other hand, our subconscious perceives it as something filthy and bad. These may be negative programs ingrained in us since childhood by our unaware parents and guardians. The lower self will not allow something it perceives as bad and will not create what it fears. If you earn money, you will soon lose it or have to give it away.

Was your childhood surrounded by love?

Did you witness your parents' love?
Did you feel like a loved child?
Do you feel worthy of being loved?

Each of us desires beautiful, pure, romantic love that lasts until death. Those who have experienced this are fortunate. However, many people are still searching, moving from partner to partner or remaining for years in loveless relationships. If your lower self associates the concept of love with pain, suffering, separations, violence — it will attract such situations into your life. Change this program, forgive, let go, stop forcing the search and perpetually waiting, and love will find you on its own.

Let's now focus on how to help ourselves.

Clearing the Path

If you have harmed or been harmed, your path of communication between selves is surely blocked. In the first case, out of a sense of guilt, in the second, from a sense of unworthiness and identifying with the victim's position. According to the teachings of Huna, there is a fundamental key phrase leading to change: Forgiveness. However, to understand why this is so crucial, let's talk for a moment about what forgiveness is. Suppose you have been hurt in the past and your subconscious still suffers, dwelling on it.

In this case, forgiveness is not about absolving someone of guilt; it's primarily about setting yourself free. It's a change in the way you perceive reality and interpret events in your life. It is not a gift for the perpetrator, but a gift for yourself. This process is actually about healing your relationship with yourself, with your lower self. You don't have to change anything in your current contacts with those who have wronged you if you don't want to.

When you live in a painful past, you're unable to move forward, you may feel that life is holding you back, even though years pass by. As if it demands you to finally forgive your parents, spouses, partners, friends, coworkers, or anyone towards whom you feel grudge, anger, or hatred. These vibrations cause you to suffer over the years, holding onto unpleasant events in your memory. They limit your development, self-satisfaction, and the joyful experience of life. They prevent you from realizing your desires and goals. They are blockades and unfavorable beliefs on the path of communication between your selves.

Do you sometimes feel that these old grievances have become part of your identity? Each of us will find a moment in our lives when everything changed. Often, this is accompanied by unpleasant experiences. If they are not transformed, they can poison our reality for a very long time. You have clung to these painful events, which perhaps happened 5, 10, or maybe 20 years ago, and you still carry them with you. You can free yourself from them, even in the case of the worst and most difficult experiences. Your painful past should not define your "here and now" because it no longer exists. You are only reanimating it in your subconscious mind and reliving it. You are stuck in a pattern of renewing it.

Have you ever asked yourself why you do this? Why do you reminisce about that time, complain, and dwell on it? You think that by doing so, you protect yourself from experiencing a traumatic blow or an unpleasant experience again.

You hold it within as "alive and fresh" to be ready. In reality, living in the past in the present moment makes the likelihood of a similar experience happening again greater, not lesser. It's your negative auto-suggestion. You can't change the past; what happened, happened. Why do you drag along something that does not serve you?

I'm not talking about forgetting; you won't forget. Your brain has an "protective system" built-in; it will sound the alarm in every similar difficult situation that you have encountered in the past. It operates on the principle of action — reaction. It does this to protect you. However, you don't have to deliberately return to difficult memories and relive them if there is no danger nearby. What once happened as a difficult experience now lives only in your head; in the real world, it does not exist, it has passed. Since the past is no more, and the future has not yet been born, we are left with the moment of "here and now." The most important and most ignored moment. Manawa, the fourth principle of Huna.

Only in the present moment can you decide to change your life or to continue following old patterns.

If you have ever been mistreated, you might believe that forgiveness is the ultimate surrender, a seal on the evil experienced: "he wronged me, and yet I forgive him." Such thinking is the biggest trap you can fall into. Forgiveness does not mean ignoring injustice or allowing someone to mistreat you. Remember, it is not a "softie's" reaction. Taking this step requires courage and effort. Letting go of your grievances requires great moral strength.

It's not the perpetrator of your grief who will live with a thorn in their heart, a sense of injustice and injury, but you. The sooner you understand this, the better for you. Forgiveness is also not about repressing pain, as that achieves nothing. When you suppress feelings, you still know you have them, but you push them away. If you try to forgive solely through a thought process, without acknowledging that you feel anger, sadness, or depression, nothing will happen.

Therefore, if you do not allow yourself to fully experience all emotions and try to suppress them, your subconscious creates situations that force you to experience them. When you wish to forgive someone or something, remember that you first had to feel anger against that person or thing. Anger is essentially a secondary emotion; underneath it lies primary pain, such as hurt pride, shame, frustration, sadness, or fear. Anger represents energy in motion, emanating from suppressed pain. Suppressing anger is like covering a volcano; one day, it will erupt!

So, what can you do yourself to forgive? You can write a letter that you will never send...

Write to the person who hurt you. Pour out all your genuine anger and all the emotions you feel, use vulgar words if you need to, scream and cry, hit the table with your fist. Get it all out, transfer everything onto paper. When you cool down, burn the paper. Watching the flame, know that what is bad is leaving, burning away. For your subconscious, this is a powerful symbol. You might repeat this after some time, and you will probably be surprised to see that each subsequent letter to that person becomes more neutral, until finally, emptiness appears. Forgiveness is not forgetting the situation that hurt you. You won't forget. You will remember the harm you suffered, but you will stop nurturing it within yourself and fueling it with anger. Your lower self will be freed from it. This is possible only when suppressed anger is acknowledged and experienced, when you recognize your injuries, when you tell yourself and admit how it was.

Therefore, forgiveness requires deep understanding; you can't just look at what's on the surface. You must consider the motives of the person who hurt you and understand what drove them. In place of long-standing injuries, new life energy will flow in, bringing with it new possibilities for further development. This will allow you to leave the past behind and focus on creation. If, however, you are someone who has caused harm or provoked a hurtful event to another being, the guilt in your lower self will prevent smooth and free communication between selves. The best course of action would be to ask for forgiveness, directly and literally. If such a situation cannot occur, you may use the method of writing a letter to your victim that you will never send (as I described above). There is also a process of cleansing from guilt, which has greatly helped my students. Check if it also speaks to you.

Exercise

Find a moment for yourself and ensure that no one will disturb you. Sit or lie down, making sure you are comfortable and warm. Close your eyes and relax. Surround yourself with a sphere of white-gold light, knowing it is the positive energy of love. It envelops you and your space. Observe your breath for a while. Search within for that emotion. Where has the feeling of guilt, shame, and regret settled? With your mind's eye, recall that moment, that person, and the situation causing the guilt. Remember everything in detail. The colors, sounds, smells, words. Experience it once again. Tears may flow, let them; these are good tears of cleansing. Now see how this entire event is bathed in white-gold, cleansing light. Feel and know that this is the positive, healing energy of love. It seeps slowly into every nook between you. Reaching everywhere, observe it. It flows into you, slowly and lovingly. You feel it even on your skin, everywhere. It dissolves all that happened just a moment ago. Bringing you closer to each other. Look into the eyes of the other person and apologize. Let it come from the area around your heart. See how he/she smiles back at you. Understood and forgiven. The relief you now feel is indescribable. You feel wonderfully light. The white-gold energy forms a sphere around that person and another around you. Calmly and safely, you return to yourself. Slowly come out of the relaxation. Notice what you now feel and give thanks for this process.

It's important to remember that our lower self revels in appeasement. Do something selflessly for another person, without seeking applause or glory. Familiarize yourself with the topics of affirmations and visualizations, powerful and underrated tools for collaborating with your subconscious. Example affirmation (you can replace "lower self" with the name you've given your subconscious): *My lower self is calm, safe, and loved. Within us, a mighty Guardian Being spreads its wings. We are one in the dance of the Universe's energy.*

Self-healing

Advice and content contained in this chapter do not absolve you from following the recommendations of a conventional medicine doctor and undergoing diagnostic tests. If you decide to make changes regarding your ailments, consult your doctor first. I mentioned earlier that our lower self always strives for homeostasis in the body. That's its task, as long as we allow it and do not disrupt this process. Unconsciously, bad habits and customs disturb this state.

Our body has cellular memory, and considering that our ancestors' diet was simpler, it is "recorded" in us how to digest an apple or a carrot. It's also worth knowing that parts of our body tend to remember their individual variants of the basic pattern. Take your skin, for example. Every day you lose millions of dead cells, only for new, identical ones to appear in their place, remembering the color of your skin and their position. Processed food stored in aluminum cans and then quickly heated in a microwave poses a significant challenge for our digestive system. Every process occurring in our body requires life energy, mana. Digesting unhealthy food requires a lot of such energy and much more time. It's a pity because this energy could be used for the repair processes of our body.

I encourage you to explore the concept of intermittent fasting, or rather, time-restricted eating. We consume meals during a specific part of the day, for example, between 12:00 PM — 5:00 PM, and then we eat nothing further. During this time, the lower self has the opportunity to allocate energy to self-repair and healing tasks. When we are in a continuous process of digesting food, energy must be redirected there, as it is a process of primary necessity. I will not delve into the subject of diet here, as it is a very individual matter. However, it is important to ensure that our meals are as balanced and nutritious as possible.

Another factor that blocks the processes of self-healing, and even causes a range of difficult diseases, is the curse of our civilization: chronic stress. Look at the changes that have taken place in our country over the last 15—20 years. Considering socio-economic progress, we should be content. But what price did we have to pay? Aggressive competition, constant rush, tension, uncertainty about tomorrow, pervasive pressure - all of these lead to prolonged, chronic stress. The danger is that we gradually get used to such a life and believe that it must be this way. We incorporate it into our daily routine. Even the so-called ability to work under stress has become an asset when applying for new employment. It is estimated that 80% of the diseases of our times have their roots in prolonged stress. Such a state can even cause damage to internal organs and many serious diseases. The greatest devastation, however, is caused by hidden, unexpressed stress, concealed for years. It most often appears in marital and family conflicts.

Living in constant tension prevents the use of mana for repair processes due to the lack of its free flow.

Practicing Huna can help you eliminate accumulated stress in your body. If you must be a participant in difficult situations at work or in other environments, you will develop the skill of being a passive observer in such moments. Initially, try not to accumulate stress energy within yourself. After a hard day, if you can, go for a run, tire yourself out intentionally with the goal of getting rid of stress. Punch a pillow in a closed room until you are tired. Just remember not to harm any other being. Taking it out on another person will not help, quite the opposite. You can also perform a breathing exercise that will release tension. It's very effective.

Exercise

When you feel overwhelmed by stress, pause for a moment. Take a slow, deep breath through your nose so that not only your chest but also your entire abdomen expands forward. Hold your breath in your lungs, counting to four. Purse your lips as if you were going to whistle and slowly release the air in a thin stream, counting to eight. Repeat this two or three times.

Through certain exercises, you can train your subconscious to activate a state of relaxation almost on demand. Remember

Ivan Pavlov's experiment? In behavioral psychology, we call this classical conditioning, which operates on the *stimulus → response principle*. It involves the creation of a connection between an innate tendency to respond and a signal that occurs together with the objective of the response. There are many everyday examples to confirm this relationship. Remember how you used to await the school bell signaling the end of a lesson? The bell became associated with rest, freedom, and the opportunity to finally do what you wanted. Its frequent ringing throughout the day solidified your response. *Bell → freedom, stimulus → response.* Another example: perhaps you know a pleasant song that emerged in your life alongside a sympathetic event? People in love often say they have "their" song, listening to it frequently. When you hear it again after many years, pleasant feelings and memories return. *Song → pleasant memories, stimulus → response.*

Our subconscious enjoys such games, so we'll use this to strengthen and induce a state of relaxation. The exercise I'm about to suggest has several advantages; you can use it anywhere and in any situation — at a friend's party, at work, during an important meeting, or conversation. Whenever you feel stress coming on. You'll use your hand, which you always have with you, regardless of where you are.

Choose a finger arrangement that suits you, it should be discreet. Something you can do anywhere, like clenching your hand into a fist or hiding the thumb between the other fingers, crossing one finger over another - try it and choose the arrangement that suits you. At this moment, your lower self does not associate this with anything, you need to teach it the appropriate reaction. Each time you consciously enter a state of relaxation and begin to feel this pleasant state — immediately arrange your hand in your chosen configuration. Gently instruct your lower self that whenever you arrange your hand in this way, it should instantly bring a state of emotional calm and tranquility. Practice this several times until your subconscious accepts the new program. You just need to teach it. You may be surprised by the positive effects. If you use your left hand for this, always use only the left hand from now on.

Illness in our body is an unnatural state. Every organ and cell in our body has the ability to regenerate and renew. If you cut your finger, your body will do everything to heal the wound as quickly as possible. We know this and believe in it, and you have probably witnessed it yourself. You can't see your internal organs, which makes it harder to have such certainty, but that doesn't change the fact that these processes occur. If an illness has already appeared, our role is to support healing, not to hinder it. Take care of yourself by considering nutrition and stress reduction, but most importantly, change the programming of your lower self. On one hand, your subconscious does everything to maintain the body's balance as it is one of its tasks, and on the other hand, you "train" it with negative programs, patterns, imaginations, thoughts about your illness. You should create a cohesive team, walking together in the same direction towards health and balance. It doesn't matter what stage of illness you are in. Your moment of power is now (manawa), all health limitations are only in your mind (kala), and all the power needed for regeneration is within you (mana).

Start cooperating with your lower self now, consciously changing the negative program that is ingrained there. Don't be surprised if your subconscious initially resists, as it is accustomed to something else. Approach this as you would teach a five-year-old, with patience and love. Praise and reward it for every small success. If doubts arise, don't succumb to them, your power is stronger than that. First, stop giving your illness great power, significance, and seriousness. Start seeing it as a pimple on the chin. I know, your subconscious is probably outraged now. After all, it's a serious illness... doctors, science, the medications you take, treatments, the books you've read on the subject, what professors say on TV, everything indicates that it's very serious... I just described the program of your lower self regarding this issue. I'm not undermining that the world of conventional medicine has diagnosed your case as serious, but did someone order you to think and be afraid like that? Remember? Your power begins where fear ends. Feel it. Put aside all negative and frightening information about the illness. Ask your loved ones not to overly sympathize with you and not to provoke conversations that stir uncertainty and fear. Don't position yourself in a battle with the illness and don't be angry at it, don't blame anyone for this state because then you give it power, you surrender your energy to it, you feed it. If possible, spend time in nature and benefit from the energy of the sun, water, air, and earth. Touch trees, especially pines and birches.

Underappreciated affirmations... I've often experienced their transformative power firsthand, both physically and in various aspects of my life. You can harness these as a tool to alter the negative programming within your deeper self. Imagine a time before your illness, when you were enveloped in joy—perhaps laughing or dancing. Present this image to your subconscious, affirming, 'I am healthy and feel fantastic.' Embrace this state, and let gratitude for this positive direction fill you.

Repeat this often, patiently guiding yourself like a nurturing teacher. Approach it with love, not force. Eventually, your inner self will replace the negative patterns with these positive affirmations. It will start to remind you of them, even craving their repetition.

If the ailment is localized, like in the liver, gently place your hands over the area. Picture a radiant white-gold light emanating from your hands, infusing the liver with healing energy. Encourage your subconscious to aid in this process.

This isn't mere fantasy. Each of us harbors such capabilities, accessible to all who seek them. Sadly, we're rarely informed about or taught these methods. Remember, you are a potent Energetic Being. It's time to reawaken to that truth.

In the upcoming chapters, you'll delve into the Huna prayer, your next step on this healing journey.

The Power of Visualization

VISUALIZATION IS AN actively engaging method where one creates multisensory images and experiences the accompanying emotions. Scientific research from the 1960s confirms its effectiveness in clinical applications. Its benefits are twofold: directly in improving health and reducing symptoms, and indirectly by enhancing well-being and quality of life.

There are two perspectives in imagery creation: internal and external observation. Effective visualization can profoundly alter your emotional state, as images directly impact your neurology. The 'lower self', when provided with these images, is inclined to act in accordance with their content. Through visualization, we change emotions or physical sensations, essentially shaping our experiences and participating in their creation. It's a natural human ability, which, when honed and focused, becomes an immensely powerful technique for achieving various goals.

To demonstrate this, consider the real-life example of Dr. Dennis Waitley's use of visualization in the 1980s, following patterns from the Apollo program. He worked with Olympic athletes, asking them to mentally rehearse sporting events. Connected to biofeedback equipment, the athletes' muscles responded during these mental exercises as if they were physically participating in the events. The measurements clearly showed muscle activity similar to that of actual physical engagement. This approach is now recognized as mental training.

The Role of Visualization

Visualization's primary role is to create a captivating and vivid image of your desires, generating powerful emotions. These emotions are key to effective visualization. The versatility of visualization is remarkable; it can boost confidence, aid in public speaking by managing stress, and facilitate personal growth.

◇ It helps build self-esteem and rectifies past errors.

◇ Aids in forgiveness and eliminating negative subconscious programming.

◇ Triggers positive moods and emotions.

◇ Develops strategies for accelerated and efficient learning.

◇ Enhances concentration.

◇ Supports healing processes.

◇ Enables mental rehearsal for overcoming challenging life situations.

◇ Strengthens skills through mental practice.

◇ Overcomes phobias, limitations, and blockages.

◇ Crucially, it allows for the rapid and effective creation of your future.

Feeling as if you already possess what you're visualizing is crucial. Often misunderstood as self-deception, this process actually starts in the 'middle self', evoking emotions from the 'lower self', which then lead to specific actions.

Focus on the end result, not the details or the 'how'. Unlike daydreaming, which is pleasant but unproductive, effective visualization involves concrete visions and effortless action, marked by freedom, decisiveness, and spontaneous joy.

Despite its name, visualization is not just visual; it's most effective when involving all senses: taste, touch, smell, sight, and hearing. Knowing which sensory channel works best for you enhances the effectiveness of your visualization. Make your images expansive, colorful, and detailed, involving as many senses as possible. This multi-sensory approach engages various brain areas, making the visualization more impactful.

The best time for visualization is right before sleep, or during deep relaxation or meditation. It's vital to be relaxed, as tension hinders the 'lower self' from effectively processing information.

How to See Internal Images?

In my work, I've often met students who believed they couldn't visualize, either seeing nothing or only blurry, distant images. To challenge this, I'd ask them to imagine something familiar and vivid. For instance, could they picture a beautiful scene or recall a detailed memory? Often, they found they could indeed visualize clearly. This shows that visualization is a natural ability of every human being.

If you haven't consciously focused on your visualizations before, it might feel new, but it's a skill you've always had. Now, it's about using this 'tool' productively and with full awareness. Here are some exercises to improve the creation of internal images:

EXERCISE 1

◈ *Choose an object in your room or environment, like a phone, monitor, or notebook.*

◈ *Place it close to you for comfortable viewing.*

◈ *Observe it for about 5 seconds, then close your eyes and visualize what you just saw.*

◈ *Try to maintain this image as long as possible.*

◈ *If the image fades, simply open your eyes and repeat. After a few tries, switch to a different object and repeat the process.*

This exercise helps you create precise images on demand. It's all about practice, and you'll find visualization becoming more natural each day.

Exercise 2

⬦ *Take a book you enjoy, randomly select a page, and start reading.*

⬦ *After a few lines, stop, close your eyes, and begin to imagine everything you just read.*

⬦ *Focus on details: the characters, setting, dialogue.*

⬦ *Visualize this scene for a minute, then return to reading.*

⬦ *Repeat this process after a few more lines.*

Books, with their rich descriptions, are excellent for developing imagination. This exercise will enhance your ability to notice and maintain detailed visualizations.

Remember, regular practice is key.

The Power of Affirmations

Many people who begin using affirmations to shape their reality do so incorrectly, yet expect the right results. Statistically, more than half give up after three months, not seeing the changes they desire. Why is this the case?

⬦ ***Lack of Emotional Alignment:*** *There's often a disconnect between the emotion and the envisioned outcome.*

◈ ***Understanding Your 'Lower Self':*** *A failure to comprehend how the 'lower self' reacts to attempts at changing reality.*

◈ ***Eliminating Negative Beliefs:*** *Many don't successfully remove the blockages and negative beliefs that hinder desired changes.*

◈ ***Subconscious Processes:*** *There's a lack of understanding of what happens in the subconscious when working with affirmations.*

◈ ***Proper Autosuggestion:*** *Absence of effective self-suggestion techniques.*

Using affirmations without understanding how they work, or applying incorrect techniques, can lead to a contradiction in belief and reality. Without awareness and self-observation, incorrect affirmations might even become harmful autohypnosis.

Randomly chosen affirmations, perhaps found online, are not a one-size-fits-all solution. They should be personalized and resonate with your current emotional state. Emotions are key in affirmation efficacy. Using a poorly formulated affirmation that doesn't resonate emotionally is destined to fail. Forcing positive thinking amidst internal doubts and fears is counterproductive.

There's a common misconception that affirmations, or personal development in general, are meant to 'fix' us, to make us more perfect. But you are already perfect in your entirety. The feeling of being incomplete or flawed only limits you. Affirmations are not about changing what is already perfect; they are about choosing a new path, a change of direction.

What are Effective Affirmations?

Effective affirmations are confirmations that you are already good enough to choose a different life path. It's about making a decision, not about fixing yourself. We all make mistakes; what's important is to learn from them, make amends, and then move forward.

Affirmations should cultivate an attitude of being an 'observer' of the changes occurring, rather than identifying with the problem. It's more effective to use your inner power rather than the force of your mind, as force often meets resistance.

When formulating affirmations, refer only to yourself, avoiding negations. Use concise statements in the past tense, and combine them with heart space and creative visualization. Then, stay in a state of free joy, avoiding control, force, or overly eager anticipation of the outcome.

The concept of Huna, which we will explore in the context of prayer, will further illuminate the process of materializing your goals.

Cyclicality

This term refers to a cycle of specific activities that are repeated regularly, either continuously or at intervals. Cyclical order is based on the constant repetition of a phenomenon. Have you ever wondered why a particular TV commercial is repeated at short intervals? Or why the same advertising posters reappear on the streets almost incessantly?

These often depict scenes designed to evoke emotions, whether positive or negative — the goal is to elicit an emotional response. The psychology of marketing understands the power of cyclicality, especially when it's intertwined with emotions. We often find ourselves in a store, inexplicably drawn to a chocolate bar or face cream we've seen advertised.

Content that is emphasized repeatedly tends to seep into our subconscious. Anything you repeat frequently — regardless of its nature — will eventually lodge in your subconscious and start to operate automatically. That's why permanent change in your life must occur at the level of the 'lower self', where enduring patterns reside and are repeated.

By practicing something long enough and learning to relinquish control, you begin to trust your subconscious. This trust can lead to surprising results — your subconscious will start functioning autonomously.

What is Prayer According to Huna?

When I first encountered prayer as taught in Huna, it seemed strange and unusual, differing significantly from the prayers of my Catholic upbringing. The routine recitation of set words, the solemn faces in church, and the ritualistic gestures contrasted starkly with my childhood experiences.

In common prayer practices, there's often an element of pleading or bargaining with God, accompanied by a litany of complaints and requests. In contrast, Huna prayer eschews artificial humility, regret, sadness, or confession of sins. There's no need for verbal patterns or even faith – just knowledge and trust in the process.

My first experience with Huna prayer brought forth emotions of peace, security, joy, love, and fulfillment – feelings I hadn't encountered in religious ceremonies. Huna teaches that prayer should be supported by knowledge and understanding. It's conscious and attentive, with an underlying joy and certainty of fulfillment. This certainty stems from understanding the process at hand.

For practicing Catholics who find solace in their faith, Huna doesn't necessitate giving anything up. It can be integrated as a form of energizing practice, relaxation, meditation, or calming exercise.

According to Huna, prayer should begin only when the path of communication between the selves is clear of blockages, rigid patterns, and negative programs. This is when you've harmonized with your lower self, understood life energy (mana), and can consciously direct it. Your higher self should be a felt presence.

Intentions in prayer should be pure and not aimed at harming or influencing others against their will. Focus on what you wish to achieve, rather than what you want to eliminate. It's a moment of solemn joy, given your full attention and focus. If there are days you don't feel like praying, don't force it. There's no need for guilt; return when you feel the desire.

Joyful anticipation is your guide to the right time for Huna prayer. You won't lose favor with your higher self by taking a break. Your prayer should have a clear goal, with either detailed or open-ended plans for your new reality.

However, start by analyzing your life and working with your subconscious to understand what is most important to you now. It's advisable to focus on one goal at a time. Pay attention to how your lower self reacts; if joy and excitement are present, you're on the right track. If doubts or feelings of unworthiness arise, revisit the seven principles of Huna and the concept of clearing the path.

If you're uncertain about what to pray for, seek inspiration from your higher self during quiet moments. Then, make a conscious decision about the form of your prayer. Your lower self will begin to act according to the knowledge and program it receives from you, with support from your higher guardian being in materializing your intentions.

I advocate flexibility in prayer; create it as you feel, ensuring it resonates with you. In the next chapter, I'll provide examples, but feel free to adapt them to suit you.

Crucially, formulate your prayers in the present tense: 'I have', 'I am', 'I possess'. Focus on a reality where the problem no longer exists, as if it has already been resolved. Avoid negations and negative imagery. Remember, the subconscious communicates through emotions and visions, so fall in love with your prayer. Show your subconscious the feelings associated with your prayer's materialization.

If your prayer involves a new job, visualize signing the contract, feeling the handshake of the CEO, or sitting in your new office chair. Immerse yourself so deeply that the lines between visualization and reality blur.

During prayer, physical sensations like tingling in the crown chakra or a rush of warmth may occur, along with a profound sense of bliss or even tears. Such experiences, especially during initial contacts with your higher self, are like reuniting with a long-lost beloved friend.

Effective Huna Prayer

When the day of your first Huna prayer arrives, start the morning with positive thoughts. Keep your subconscious in joyful anticipation, like a child eagerly awaiting Christmas Eve. This time is solely for you; ensure your surroundings are peaceful. A piece of relaxing music can help set the mood, playing quietly in the background.

1. *Assume a Comfortable Position*: Ensure your spine is straight and that you're warm, as feeling cold can distract your lower self. Most of my students prefer lying down under a warm blanket.

2. *Relax Your Body*: Close your eyes and focus on feeling your body relax. Imagine any tension leaving your body like evaporating mist, harmlessly dissipating.

3. *Acknowledge Your Thoughts*: Allow any thoughts to surface without fighting them. Observe them from a distance as you envelop yourself in a sphere of white-gold light, symbolizing positive, loving energy.

4. *Visualize a Sphere*: Imagine a transparent, light sphere, the size of a melon, floating above you at navel level. Speak to your lower self, either in thoughts or aloud: "We are ready to send our prayer to our higher self. You will fill this sphere with mana and our new reality. With each breath, energy will flow into it."

5. *Observe Your Breath*: Let your breathing be natural. Visualize each breath filling the sphere with golden energy. Continue until it feels complete.

6. *Enter the Sphere with Visualization*: Look at the sphere, now filled with images. If your prayer is about buying a new house, see and experience it within this sphere. Feel the textures, hear the sounds, and immerse yourself in this new reality.

7. *Return to Your Body*: Imagine your body returning to its normal size. You are back under the blanket, with the sphere of your desires floating above.

8. ***Send the Sphere to Your Higher Self****: Tell your subconscious to send the sphere upward, filled with love and joy. Visualize it rising higher until it disappears.*

9. ***Focus on the Crown Chakra****: Direct your attention to the top of your head. Open yourself to contact with your higher self, inviting its active participation, guidance, and support in your life.*

After a moment of silence, express gratitude to your lower self for its work and marvel at the contact made with your higher self.

This description outlines my approach to Huna prayer. Remember, you can adapt it to resonate with your feelings and judgment. Key elements include transmitting mana and mental images with emotional content to your higher self.

It's recommended to send the prayer three times, not necessarily on consecutive days, but without long breaks. If there are physical actions you can take towards realizing your prayer, do so. Be open to 'miraculous coincidences' and the inspirations of your higher self.

Anchoring

HUNA REPRESENTS A REMARKABLE journey into oneself. By incorporating it into your daily life, you'll notice a transformation in your lifestyle. You'll start to see reality differently and, most importantly, reclaim your innate power of creation – a natural right of every human being.

Huna comprises a series of suggestions, tips, and techniques aimed at developing consciousness and regaining the fullness of one's being. This is achieved through the symbiosis of the selves and understanding simple principles. Rather than forcing yourself to learn these concepts, embrace them. Experiment, discover, and experience.

True, initial efforts to change negative subconscious patterns and habits require patience and self-discipline. However, taking control of your life's creation, enhancing mental and physical health, refining your character, and achieving inner peace, harmony, and a sense of security are well worth these efforts.

Daily, nourish yourself with life energy, or 'mana'. A few conscious, deep breaths each evening are enough. Request your lower self to distribute this energy to the parts of you that need it the most.

Reconnecting with your higher self brings about an unwavering sense of security, not just trust, but certainty – akin to the certainty that another day will follow.

When sending a prayer to your higher self, transmit your vision but refrain from forcing a specific scenario. Loosen your grip on controlling the situation. Avoid overthinking the development of events. You can't predict all the movements of the universe or know exactly how your goal will manifest. Be open to new options and possibilities that might currently be unseen or unconsidered.

Maintain the vision of a new you or a new reality. Embrace the principles of Huna as part of your daily routine, and live in the spirit of Aloha :)

List of Sources and Literature:
A. Holub, "The Power of Forgiveness," Illuminatio, 2015
G. Braden, "The Isaiah Effect," Studio Astropsychologii, 2011
M.F. Long, "Autosuggestion," Wydawnictwo Medium, 1995
M.F. Long, "The Magic of Miracles," Wydawnictwo Medium, 1995

Don't miss out!

Visit the website below and you can sign up to receive emails whenever Katarzyna Biedrzycka publishes a new book. There's no charge and no obligation.

https://books2read.com/r/B-A-RXXCB-QZIUC

BOOKS 2 READ

Connecting independent readers to independent writers.

About the Author

Katarzyna Biedrzycka — a personal trainer, coach, author of books and publications. She conducts efficiency workshops in the field of professional and personal development, goal achievement, stress management, and improving the quality of life across its various aspects. In her work, she utilizes the knowledge and wisdom of Huna, as well as relaxation and meditation techniques, as effective tools for practicing the principles of the limitless power of the human mind, upon which our life in this reality is based.

www.ingramcontent.com/pod-product-compliance
Lightning Source LLC
Chambersburg PA
CBHW051458140726
47987CB00006B/2764